here to 🐝 seen

g h anonymous

HERE TO BE SEEN

published by IPBooks, Queens, NY

ISBN: 978-1-956864-53-3

Master Teachers

Thank You

Mr. Maloof
André and Pierre Brunet
Nina Stroganova
&
Vladimir Dokoudovsky

Franz Peter Schubert

"Fantasia in F minor"

this book was created using three
iPhones set up to intercommunicate

one was an active iPhone 12 Mini
another an old iPhone 12 Mini
a third a new iPhone 14 Plus
which approximated the picture size
of pages I envisioned for the book

the capabilities of the phones were
explored and manipulated through
multiple haptic maneuvers into
curated single page images that pop
up intact when opened on an iPhone

each page is unique

iPhone as iBook

"Hey GPS
          let's take the scenic route"

"We're almost there
          but nowhere near it"

"I am a Tralfamadorian,
seeing all time as you might see a
stretch of the Rocky Mountains. All
time is all time. It does not change.
It does not lend itself to warnings or
explanations".

Kurt Vonnegut

Wunderbares Bild

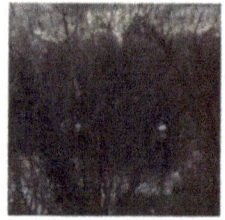

Creativity is just connecting things. When you ask creative people how they did something, they feel a little guilty because they didn't really do it, they just saw something. It seemed obvious to them after a while. That's because they were able to connect experiences they've had and synthesize new things.

Steve Jobs

66 Thus, the task is not so much
to see what no one yet has
seen, but to think what nobody
yet has thought about that
which everybody sees.

Arthur Schopenhauer

BUSH

inside the bush

Lily's Schtick

According to Lewis, "actual" is merely an indexical label we give a world when we are in it.

An Ancient Evergreen, dancing in
a winter breeze, captured an Angel
reflected in a window of the Lounge
in the Grand Hotel Hof Ragaz.

Once the realization is accepted that
even between the closest human
beings infinite distances continue. a
wonderful living side by side can grow. if
they succeed in loving the distance
between them which makes it possible
for each to see the other whole against
the sky.
Rainer Maria Rilke

"One does not fall in love, one
grows into love and love grows in
him"

Karl Menninger

Mozart: Piano Concertos No.21 K.467
II.Andante Géza Anda/piano (1961) Elvira
Madigan (1967)

HISTORY
Berlin 1945

**20 years after the fall of
the wall | Peter Eisenmans
Holocaust Memorial**

"Take a deep breath, spread your wings, and fly." - Unknown.

Quote of the day

"In nature there are neither rewards
or punishments there are
consequences "

Robert Ingersoll

Re: : Quote of the day

Ingersoll statue in Peoria, Illinois

◆ "May he stand in Peace" ◆

Quote for today

"A good photograph is knowing
where to stand ".
Ansel Adams

Archimedes of Syracuse (c. 287 BC –
c. 212 BC) was a Greek mathematician,
philosopher, scientist and engineer.

Give me a place to stand, and I
shall move the world.

?

it is what it is

it was what it was

((🔔))

Alice is the protagonist of the story. She is the main character and everything evolves around her. We follow her during her trip through Wonderland and know what she is thinking.

SHELF LIFE

Each was born
in His / Her Time
in a Place
in "Once upon a Time"

each is born
in their own time
in a place
once upon a time

Burnt Norton by T.S. Eliot

what might it feel
to be
trapped
in
deception
free
to see
truth
in
light
of
reflection

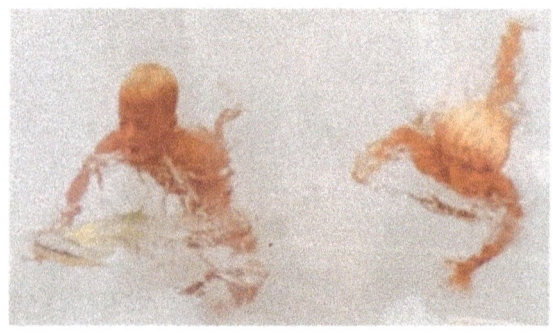

Quote for today

"What shapes the artist is the
power to shape the material of pain
that we all have"

Lionel Trilling

Life
in contrast and harmony
is woven

weft over warp
day after day
year upon year
until

at last

a tapestry
is knit.

ABOUT DONKEYS

Elephants are calling for help:

January 6, 2021
10:00 PM   Edit

♜
CAPITOL
stairs
stairs   stairs
stairs   crowd   stairs
stairs crowd   crowd stairs
crowds crowds crowds crowds

wait
wait
wait
wait
wait
wait
wait
wait
wait

they will get hungry and thirsty
and have to go to the bathroom

TODAY'S COVER
Sunday, January, 10, 2021

The word golem typically describes an animated being made from clay or mud. **There are no categorical synonyms for this word.** However, one could loosely use automaton as a synonym.

"The project must remain a torso disavowed by its creator."

(Freud)

Some golems may be human in appearance, whereas others will still resemble the material they were constructed out of. This is largely a result of how adept its creator is. Golems that resemble humans, no matter how exact their appearance is, will not have a belly button.

"descent"

// from the extremest
upward of thy head to the
descent and dust below
thy foot
— Shakespeare

THIS LAND IS MY LAND

♪ ♪ ♪ ♪ ♪ ♪

Pyrrhic
victory 🔊

Victory at a cost
tantamount to defeat

And I don't think that government has a role in telling people how to live their lives. Maybe a minister does, maybe your belief in God does, maybe there's another set of moral codes, but I don't think government has a role.

Clarence Thomas

UP

DOWN   SIDEWAYS

          DOWN

          DOWN   SIDEWAYS

                              UP

                DOWN

THING

Subject: 🗣"Wrapping"

Words are born pennies
nickels
or dimes

more or less valued
depending on times

((🐝))

🔲 2 🐝
I 2 🐝 U 2 🐝 HE 2 🐝 SHE 2 🐝 IT 2
🐝 WE 2 🐝 U 2 🐝 THEY 2 🐝 U 2

I 2 🐝
        U 2 🐝

                HE 2 🐝
    SHE 2 🐝
                IT 2 🐝

        WE 2 🐝
                    U 2 🐝
    THEY 2 🐝 U 2

Für Lily

 to write

 to compose

 to sing

🎶 your songs

❤️ yourself

 GG A G F G   🗣️ la la Lily la loo
EE F E D E   la la Lily la lee
CC DD   la la Lily
EE GG   la la Lily
GG F E D C   la la Lily la loo

deep

deeper

deepest

too deep

↑
TOP

Subject: **?**

PERSON

人

PEOPLE

人

JUST DESSERTS

CONFIGURATIONS
OF A BINARY TILE
IN A NINE SQUARE GRID

Intersectionality

Neighborhood Fem.

NYC
June 8, 2023

2022

Subject:

To doubt everything, or, to believe everything, are two equally convenient solutions; both dispense with the necessity of reflection.

Henri Poincare

f   🐦   in

Henri Poincaré was a mathematical genius who made the greatest advances in celestial mechanics since the time of Isaac Newton

Poincaré gave the first mathematical description of a dynamic system behaving chaotically.

reflection in reflection
in the vending machine
of life

(( ))